The Art of
MUSCLE

The Art of

Photography by Michael Neveux
Text by David Prokop

MUSCLE

LONGMEADOW
P R E S S

PAGE 1: Brian Buchanan/Rimini, Italy/1989
PAGE 2: Ellen Van Maris/Studio, New York City/1989
PAGE 3: Berry DeMey/Hawaii/1984
PAGE 4: Mike Christian/Venice, CA/1988

Copyright ©1994 by Brompton Books Corporation

Published by Longmeadow Press, 201 High Ridge Road, Stamford, CT 06904.

Book design by Michael Neveux
Graphic design by Leon Bach

ISBN 0-681-00578-5

Printed in Slovenia

First Longmeadow Press Edition

0 9 8 7 6 5 4 3 2 1

DEDICATION

To my beautiful wife Janice — thank you for always being so understanding and supportive, and for being my best friend.

ACKNOWLEDGMENTS

Special thanks to David Prokop for his superb writing skills, John Balik for giving me complete creative freedom with *IRONMAN* magazine which has brought about most of these images, the bodybuilders for the great physiques which continually inspire me, and my mom and dad — because without the magical mix of their genes, I wouldn't be doing this book.

CONTENTS

FOREWORD

I've always been inspired by heroic figures, which helps explain why I became involved with bodybuilding in the first place — initially as a participant, when I started weight training while still in high school, and later as a professional photographer. For me, this book is a long-awaited chance to show some of my favorite images of these modern-day gladiators with the mythical bodies that I've always found so intriguing. Of course, any photographer would welcome the opportunity to have his best work on a subject displayed in a volume such as this, but on a broader perspective I think a book showing the artistry of bodybuilding is long overdue — from the standpoint of bodybuilding itself. As you look through this book, I trust you'll agree with me. What these people have achieved is art, and it deserves to be presented and recorded as art.

My work as a physique photographer has allowed me to travel to numerous countries and meet some of the most remarkable individuals on this planet. I've also been fortunate to become associated with *IRONMAN* magazine, and through that association I've been able to create many unique photographs of these extraordinary men and women. What you see here is a large selection of my favorite bodybuilding images.

Michael Neveux

INTRODUCTION

Man has always been fascinated by art and perfection, strength and heroism, challenge and achievement.

Small wonder, therefore, that the human physique, developed to its muscular, aesthetic ultimate, has stirred something deep within us from ancient times to the present. For such a physique represents, simultaneously and undeniably, all of the above — art, perfection, strength, heroism, challenge (successfully met) and achievement. It's the most personal manifestation of man's search for physical excellence and, consequently, one of the highest possible expressions of humanity. The sport of bodybuilding is the art of muscle.

The great sculptors of the Renaissance — Michelangelo, Pollaiuolo and Gianbologna — all produced exquisite works glorifying the aesthetics of the human body. Since weight training, physical fitness and the body beautiful were hardly in vogue in 15th- and 16th-century Europe, these artists modeled their masterpieces on the classical ideal of Greek and Roman times (hence the name "Renaissance" — a humanistic revival of the ideals of the Greek and Roman classical period). Michelangelo's "David" is the artist's representation of the ideal male form. If Michelangelo were alive today, he would have as models some of the bodybuilders you see pictured on these pages.

While it is true that the ancient Greeks were the first to extol and appreciate the virtues of an aesthetic, beautiful physique — the original Olympic motto lauded "a sound mind and a healthy body" — the activity in gyms across America today, coupled with the transformation in public attitude created by the media, indicates that we are living now in what might be termed the golden age of muscle. How inspiring that the physical ideal born centuries ago in Greece and immortalized by the Renaissance masters has only now come to full flower as never before in history! Ancient mythology was once the source for such superhuman symbols of strength and physical capability as Hercules, Achilles and Atalanta, but we no longer need to look to mythology for such figures. We have living, breathing superhumans right among us. They're called bodybuilders.

Bodybuilding as we know it (training with weights to

increase strength and build the muscles) could be said to have originated with professional strongmen and weightlifters in the late 1800s. At the turn of the century there were many such individuals performing on the stage and in circus sideshows. The emphasis in their training was almost entirely on strength rather than aesthetics.

Modern bodybuilding, in which the emphasis shifted to the aesthetics of the physique, originated in the 1940s. The first great bodybuilder of the modern era was John Grimek, who, ironically, considered himself a weightlifter rather than a bodybuilder. He had been an artists' model for several years before competing as a weightlifter in the 1936 Olympics. His aesthetic lines, dense, fully developed muscles and dramatic posing set the standard in those early days of the new sport/art form.

Others soon followed, in ever increasing numbers. Since those pioneering days of the 1940s, bodybuilding has become a much more sophisticated, competitive and popular sport — with numerous competitions, for men and women, all over the country and around the world. The International Federation of Bodybuilders (IFBB), the world governing body of the sport, now boasts more than 130 member nations. Go to any large newsstand and you'll see at least five or six magazines devoted to the sport. The finest bodybuilders compete in such events as the U.S. Nationals, the Mr. Universe contest, and the greatest competition of them all — the Mr. Olympia (for men) and the Ms. Olympia (for women).

Austrian-born Arnold Schwarzenegger, now a Hollywood superstar, won seven Mr. Olympia titles from 1970 to 1980 and is regarded as the Babe Ruth of the sport. If Schwarzenegger is the Babe Ruth of bodybuilding, Lee Haney of Atlanta, Georgia, is clearly the Hank Aaron — from 1984 to 1991 Haney won eight consecutive Mr. Olympia titles, surpassing even Schwarzenegger's remarkable achievement. Cory Everson, originally from Wisconsin, is the most decorated female bodybuilder in history, having won six consecutive Ms. Olympia titles from 1984 to 1989.

The history of bodybuilding since the formative John Grimek era is filled with names that are synonymous with remarkable physique development: Clarence Ross, Steve Reeves, Reg Park, Larry Scott, Harold Poole, Dave Draper, Bill Pearl, Sergio Oliva, Arnold Schwarzenegger, Frank Zane, Franco Columbu, Serge Nubret, Chris Dickerson, Mike

Mentzer, Tom Platz, Lou Ferrigno, Boyer Coe, Samir Bannout, Lee Haney, Dorian Yates — and on the women's side of the sport, Rachel McLish, Kiki Elomaa, Carla Dunlap, Diana Dennis, Cory Everson, Bev Francis and Lenda Murray. To the serious bodybuilder, their names are as familiar as Joe Dimaggio, Willie Mays and Mickey Mantle are to baseball fans.

How the top bodybuilders are able to develop such extraordinarily aesthetic, muscular bodies is basically a function of sophisticated, systematic weight training and intelligent nutrition. By doing a wide variety of resistance exercises, either with free weights (barbells, dumbbells) or exercise machines (such as Nautilus), an individual can ultimately tone, shape and develop each muscle of the body to its fullest potential. By also incorporating aerobic exercise into the training program to burn extra calories and by paying strict attention to nutrition (consuming primarily high-fiber, low-calorie foods and cutting down on the intake of sugar and fat), it's possible to achieve the exceptional leanness necessary to show off the muscles to the best advantage. Obviously, some people have more genetic potential than others to build bigger and shapelier muscles, but the important point is that consistent weight training and sound nutrition can enable almost anyone to create an aesthetic physique, in much the same way as a sculptor would create a statue. The only difference is that a sculptor works on clay or stone, whereas the bodybuilder works on his or her own body.

Today in America muscle is accepted as never before, and its popularity is growing worldwide. Muscle is attractive, muscle is sexy, muscle is desirable, muscle is in! You see it everywhere — in the crowded gyms, in TV commercials, feature films and magazines, on the beaches, on nightclub dance floors and in the streets. Some of the biggest movie stars of the 1990s rely as much on muscle and heroic feats as they do on acting ability — Sylvester Stallone, Arnold Schwarzenegger, Chuck Norris, Jean-Claude Van Damme. That, in itself, tells us a lot about what the public wants and appreciates.

This unprecedented evolution of bodybuilding to its present popularity has been marked by several key events over the last 40 years. In chronological order, they are:

* Strikingly handsome, remarkably muscled Steve Reeves, a former Mr. Universe, stars in a series of highly profitable,

Italian-made movies in the 1950s (*Hercules, Hercules Unchained, Thief of Baghdad*), becoming the world's number-one box-office star in 1959. Reeves, now in his 60s and retired from acting, is still regarded as the greatest combination of physique excellence and facial good looks ever seen on screen or off.

* *Pumping Iron*, the 1976 film documentary produced by Charles Gaines and George Butler, introduces the bodybuilding subculture to a mass audience and signals the first real step to cinematic stardom for the film's charismatic central figure, Arnold Schwarzenegger.

* Also in the 1970s, America undergoes a consciousness transformation resulting in the fitness craze. At first the most popular form of exercise is aerobics (jogging, cycling, swimming), but in the 1980s and 1990s weight training and bodybuilding proliferates.

* Finally, in the 1990s the media (films, television, advertising, magazines) begins to focus on muscle as never before, drawing even more people to weight training and resulting in the widespread popularity bodybuilding now enjoys.

Today there are an estimated 25,000 gyms and health clubs in the United States alone, and more than 35 million people weight train at home or in gyms and health clubs. Bodybuilding has become a billion-dollar industry in America, and a multi-billion-dollar industry worldwide.

To be sure, most of the people who weight train are concerned with relatively modest aesthetic goals, but there exists a hardcore nucleus that chooses to take the training and nutritional rigors to the ultimate of physical potential. These are the people who have made their bodies a personal, private work of art, their training a never-ending labor of love, and they're proud to call themselves "bodybuilders." Some compete in contests; all compete with themselves, constantly striving to become a little better than they were the day before. A poet has written of their lifestyle and mentality: "I am a bodybuilder, I am an artist; they are one and the same to me."

Welcome to the world of bodybuilding and the art of muscle, so dramatically revealed here in the breathtaking photography of Michael Neveux.

TRAIN

Bob Paris/Calf Raise

J.J. Marsh/Dumbbell Press

Tonya Knight/Pulldown

Muscles straining, veins bulging, body glistening with sweat. A bodybuilder's training may seem — at a glance — nothing but hard work. Yet that is true only when viewed on a superficial level. "No pain, no gain" goes the slogan, but to a bodybuilder the training is more exaltation than pain, more spiritual experience than physical discomfort. On the deepest level it is as much an exercise in intense mental concentration as in maximum physical exertion — and what it produces is

a oneness of mind, body and spirit. It is, as one bodybuilder has described it, "a communion with self." And the driving force behind all this effort and commitment is a strong orienting vision. That's what it takes to test oneself against the weights day after day, to carve and shape and sculpt the body until it verges on human perfection. The serious bodybuilder is his own dream literally coming true in front of his eyes through the relentless process of pitting muscle against iron.

Paul DeMayo/Cable Curl

Kevin Hall/Leg Raise

Mike Matarazzo/Dumbbell Row

Ron Matz/Cable Curl/1989

Francois Gay/Front Chin/1992

Tom Platz/Barbell Row/1984

Mohamed Makkawy/Lying Rear Delt Raise/1983

Mike Quinn/Armblaster Barbell Curl/1989

Milos Sarcev/One-arm Dumbbell Row/1992

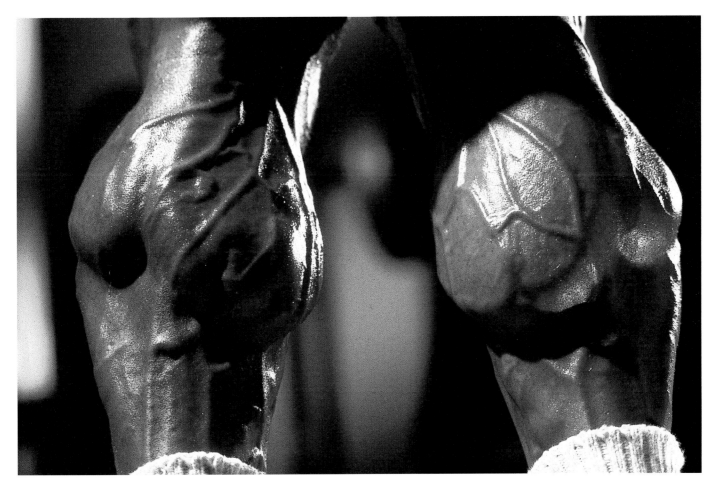

Paul DeMayo/Calf Raise/1992

Jacques Neuville/Pec Deck/1984

Mae Mollica(top), Diana Dennis/Donkey Calf Raises/1984

Jim Quinn/Shrugs/1991

Sandy Riddell/Barbell Curl/1991

Bertil Fox/Triceps Push-down/1986

Lee Haney/Mr. Olympia/Low-cable Row/1991

Rick Valente/Gold's Gym/1984

COMPE

Chris Dickerson/1984

Alanna Partipillo/1989

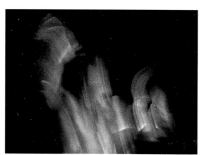

Jacques Neville/1986

After the endless months (or even years) of arduous training, to which is added weeks of stringent dieting at the end to strip the body of all excess fat so the hard-earned muscles show in every striated detail, comes the competitive bodybuilder's moment of truth — the physique contest. Here the bodybuilder will find out how good he or she really is compared to others who have undertaken the same heroic quest for physical perfection. If you're a competitive bodybuilder, the contest is showtime/opening night on Broadway/the Academy Awards all rolled into one — only more personal-

TITION

ly challenging and intimately revealing, because that's *you* up there, practically naked, and you've willingly offered yourself up for evaluation — and ultimate validation or rejection by the judges and audience alike. But when you hit them with your best shot and touch them where they live, and the roar of approval and adulation from the audience comes rolling back towards you like a tidal wave, washing over you, filling your veins with adrenalized rapture, it is the greatest rush you can experience. One such moment makes every moment of training and dieting worthwhile.

Women's Nationals/1988

Mr. Olympia/Posedown/1985

Sergio Oliva/Mr. Olympia/1984

Sean Jenkins/Men's Nationals/1986

Mary Ann Duffy/Women's Nationals/1983

Bertil Fox/Essen, Germany/1986

Lee Haney, Frank Zane, Mohamed Makkawy/Mr. Olympia contest/Munich, Germany/1983

Scott Wilson/European Tour/1983

Tara Dodane/Women's Nationals/1988

Posedown/Essen, Germany/1986

Women's Nationals/Los Angeles/1990

Jeff Williams/Men's Nationals/Las Vegas, NV/1984

Sergio Oliva/Mr. Olympia/Mr. Olympia contest, New York City/1984

Abdominals

Biceps

Rear Double Biceps

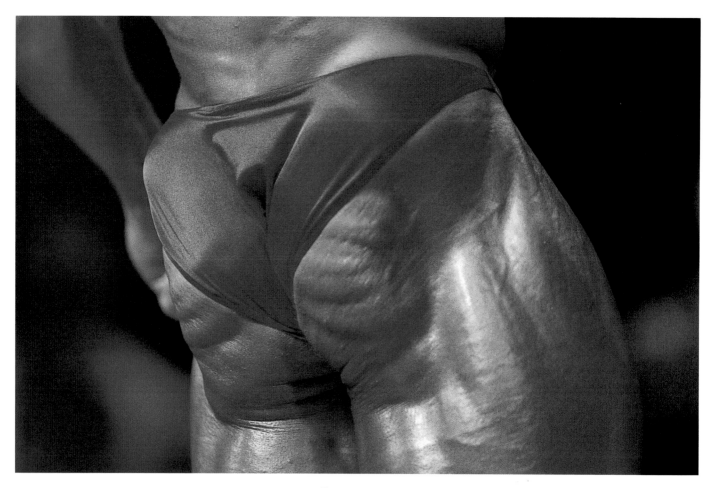

Gluteus maximus

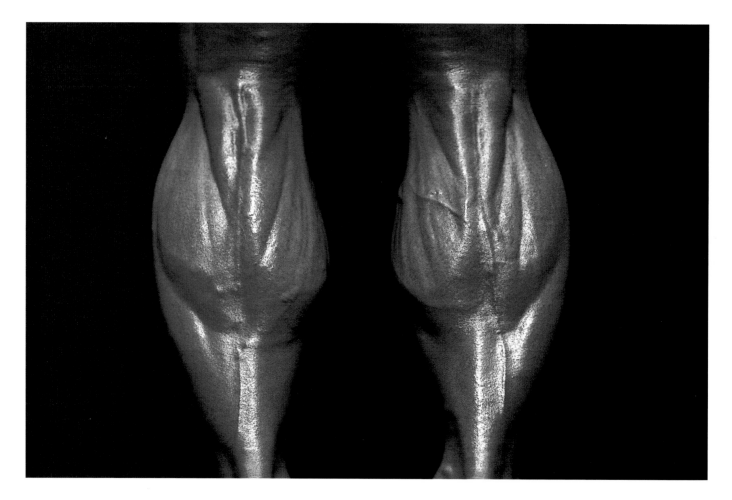

Gastrocnemius

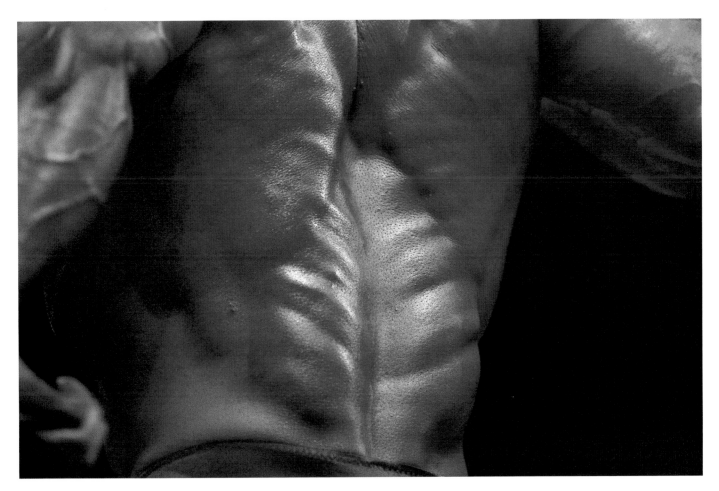

Spinal Erectors

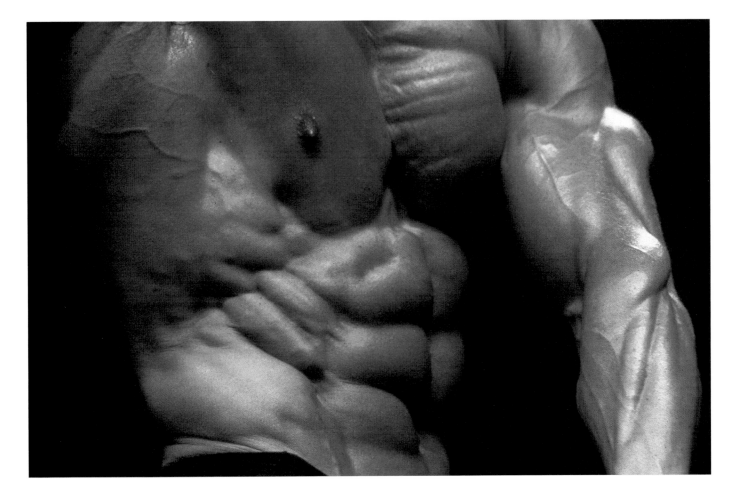

Intercostals

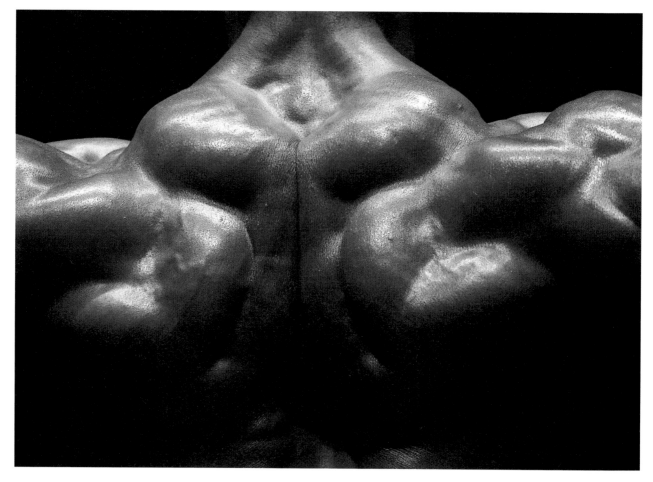

Trapezius

Deltoid

Triceps

Biceps

Renee Casella/Trapezius and Triceps

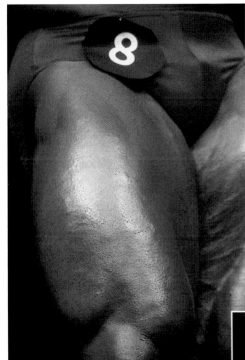

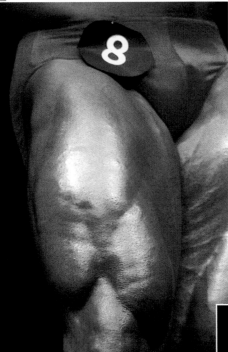

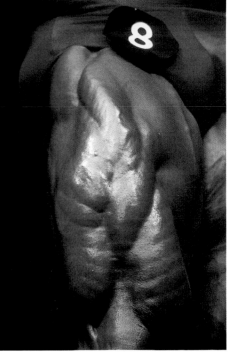

PHYS

Andre Bilodeau/1991

Kathy Unger/1990

Berry DeMey/1985

Life lived well is a constant process of being and becoming, of dreams supported by the effort to make them come true. This is the bodybuilder's particular stock-in-trade. It is the language he speaks; these are the emotions he feels. They are at once poetic and artistic emotions, filled with passion and soaring aspiration. The bodybuilder is at the same time athlete and artist, but in the studio in front of the photographer's camera, he is pure artist unveiling his work of art in all its

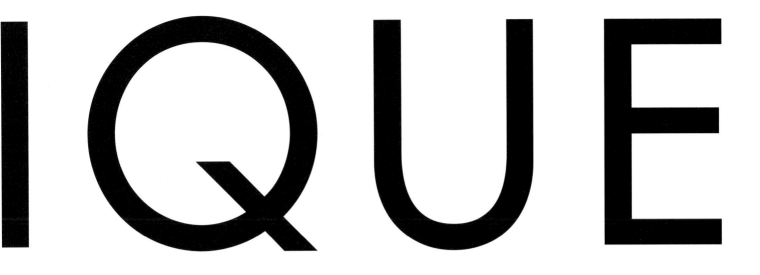

IQUE

glory. And when you get the right bodybuilder together with the right photographer, the art produced transcends the bodybuilder's individual achievement, for the photographer brings his own unique vision to the process. The result is a freeze frame captured for eternity of man or woman at his or her physical best. It is an image that is timeless, dramatic, inspiring—a true work of art.

Francis Benfatto/1990

Jackie Paisley/1987

Ken Passariello/1984

Arnold Schwarzenegger/ Mr. Olympia/Santa Monica, CA/1984

Cory Everson/Ms. Olympia/Studio, L.A./1989

Lee Haney/Mr. Olympia/New York City/1983

Francis Benfatto/Rimini, Italy/1989

Phil Hill/New York City/1988

Tom Platz/Studio, L.A./1983

Janice Ragain/Studio, L.A./1988

Bob Paris/Studio, L.A./1988

Lenda Murray/Ms. Olympia/Studio, New York City/1990

Candy Csencsits/Studio, L.A./1983

Lee Labrada/Palos Verdes, CA/1988

Franco Santoriello/Atlanta, GA/1989

Jennifer Cummings/Miami, FL/1987

John Hnatyschak/Las Vegas/1984

Thierry Pastel/New York City/1992

Roger Stewart/Studio, L.A./1992

Dennis Newman/Studio, L.A./1993

Tony Pearson/Studio, L.A./1988

Cory Everson/Ms.Olympia/Studio,LA/1987

Kevin Levrone/Pittsburgh, PA/1991

Ricardo Gya and Savannah Rose Neveux/Studio, L.A./1991

Diana Dennis/Studio, L.A./1984

Tonya Knight/Studio, L.A./1988

Dean Caputo/Los Angeles/1993

Marjo Selin/Studio, New York City/1987

Brian Buchanan/Rimini, Italy/1989

Vince Taylor/New York City/1989

Albert Beckles/New York City/1988

Carla Dunlap/Ms. Olympia/Studio, L.A./1984

Jackie Paisley/Studio, L.A./1989

Phil Hill/New York City/1988

Mary Roberts/Hawaii/1984

Frank Zane/Mr. Olympia/Palm Springs, CA/1985